Windows Magic

Claire Pye and Ruth Cassidy

W
FRANKLIN WATTS
LONDON • SYDNEY

First published in 2003 by:
Franklin Watts
96 Leonard Street
London EC2A 4XD

Franklin Watts Australia
45-51 Huntley Street
Alexandria
NSW 2015

© Franklin Watts 2003

Created by:
act-two
346 Old Street
London EC1V 9RB
www.act-two.com

Text: Ruth Cassidy
Consultant: John Siraj-Blatchford
Managing editor: Claire Pye
Editor: Deborah Kespert
Designers: Ariadne Boyle, Tim Clear
Illustrators: Ian Cunliffe, Andrew Peters
Art director: Belinda Webster
Editorial director: Jane Wilsher

A CIP catalogue record for this book
is available from the British Library.

ISBN 0 7496 4856 2

Printed in Hong Kong, China

Contents

Words marked in **bold** in the
text are explained on page 32.

How to use this book
Look at the pictures in this book
to find out what's happening on
your computer screen.

Follow each numbered step in
the book and on your computer.

1 Click on the Start button.

Coloured arrows show
you where to look on
your computer screen.

Words that are
underlined tell you
what to do next.

Your tools

Every time you work on your computer, you use a **computer program** called Windows. Its job is to make running your computer easy.

Desktop
The first thing you see when you switch on your computer is the Desktop. It's like a real desk, with folders for your work and even a bin! Desktops can be different colours. What colour is yours?

Folder
This is a **folder**. It's called the My Documents folder. You can store all your work in it, just like a real folder.

Recycle Bin
Keep your desktop tidy! Just throw away work you don't need any more, straight into the Recycle Bin.

Cursor

When you move your mouse around, a shape moves on your computer screen. It's called a **cursor**. Our cursor is shaped like an arrow, but it can change shape. What shape is your cursor?

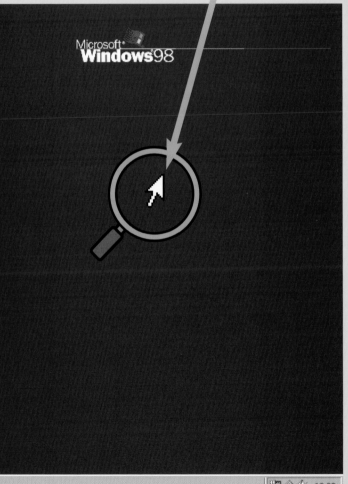

In this book, you'll need to move your cursor and click with your mouse. Here are the different ways of clicking.

Click
Press the left button on your mouse, once.

Double-click
Press the left button twice, quickly.

Drag
Press the left button and move the mouse at the same time.

Right-click
Press the right button, once.

Time to start

The Start button is an important part of Windows. Let's find out what's hiding behind it!

1 First, point your **cursor** at the Start button and click.

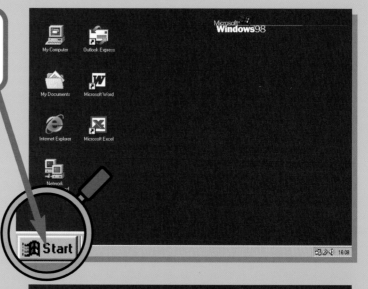

Hey presto!

Quick start!

Is there a button like this 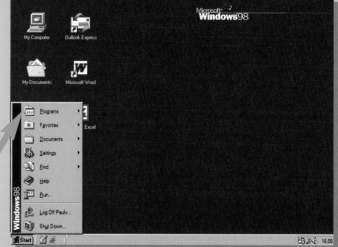 on your keyboard? It's called the Windows button. You can press it to open the Start menu.

2 This list is called a **menu**. Move your cursor up to Programs. What happens?

3 A new menu pops up! Now move your cursor over Accessories.

4 This menu contains lots of useful **computer programs**. Click on the WordPad program.

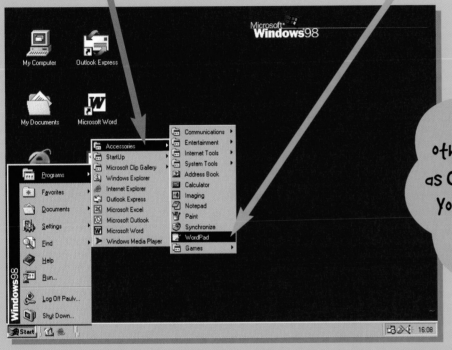

Try opening other programs, such as Calculator or Paint. You might even find some games!

5 WordPad is a computer program for typing messages or letters. You'll find out more about it on the next page.

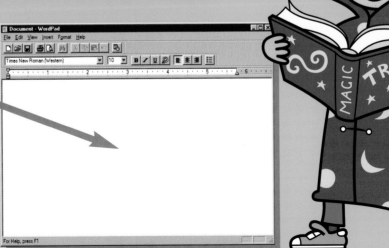

7

Save your work

Let's write a magic message in WordPad and then save it in the My Documents **folder**.

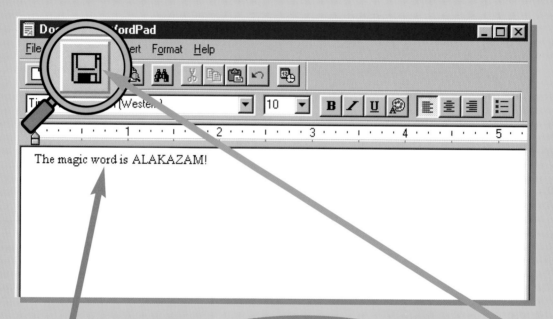

File ~~Insert~~ F~~o~~rmat ~~H~~elp

10   **B** *I* U

· · · 1 · · · | · · · 2 · · · | · · · 3 · · · | · · · 4 · · · | · · · 5 ·

The magic word is ALAKAZAM!

1 Use your keyboard to type a message. You can copy our message or make up one of your own.

Hey presto!

Capital letters trick

To type a capital letter, such as A, press the Shift key ⇧ and the letter 'A' at the same time. Try typing these capital letters: B C D.

2 Now it's time to save your message. Find this Save button and click on it.

8

3 Let's save this message in the My Documents folder.

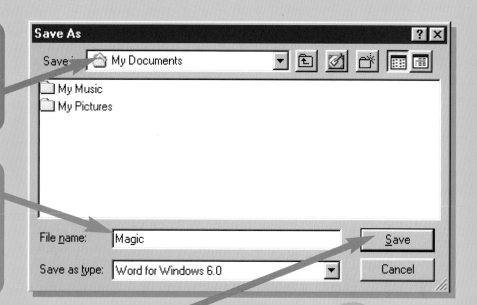

Save As

Save: My Documents

My Music
My Pictures

File name: Magic

Save as type: Word for Windows 6.0

Save

Cancel

4 Type a name for your message. We've typed the name 'Magic'.

5 You're ready to save! Click the Save button.

Try making up more magic messages in WordPad! Can you type a spell or a secret code?

6 You can see the name of your message here.

7 Now close WordPad by clicking this Close button.

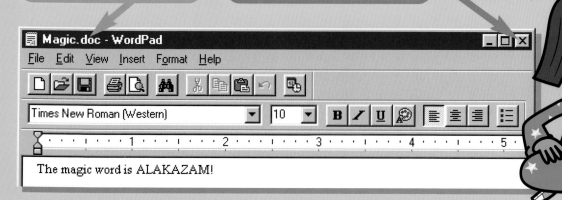

Magic.doc - WordPad

File Edit View Insert Format Help

Times New Roman (Western)   10   B I U

The magic word is ALAKAZAM!

9

Open My Documents

It's time to find your magic message again
by opening the My Documents **folder**.

1 Point your **cursor** at
the My Documents folder
and double-click.

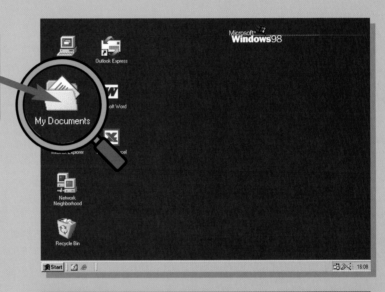

2 The folder opens so you
can see what's inside. This
big box is called a **window**.

3 Can you see the
message you have saved?

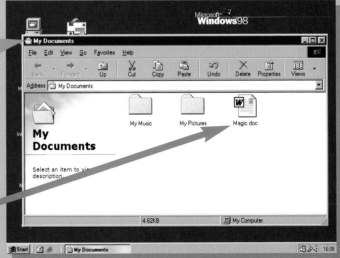

4 Let's move this window out of the way! <u>Click on this blue bar and hold down your left mouse button. Move your mouse to drag the window.</u>

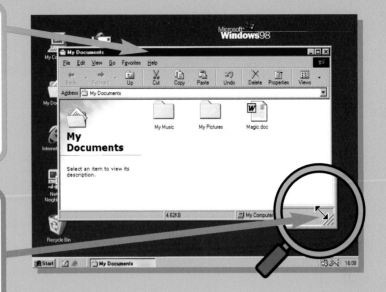

5 You can also make your window bigger or smaller. <u>Point your cursor at this corner. It turns into an arrow with two points</u>!

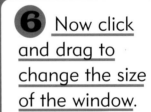

6 <u>Now click and drag to change the size of the window.</u>

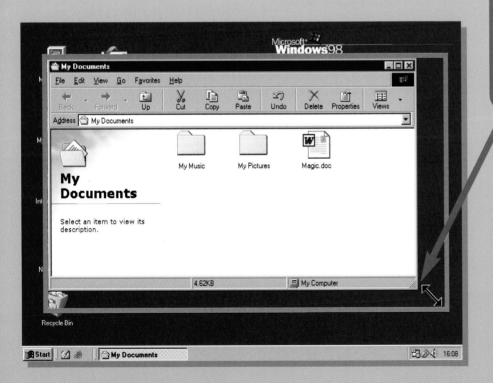

11

Up and down

Here are a few tricks to make windows grow, shrink, and even hide.

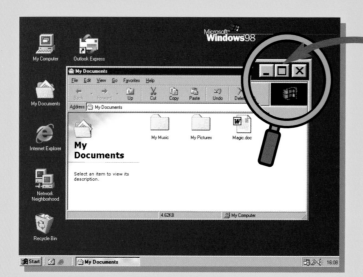

1 Let's take a closer look at this window. <u>Find the Maximize button and click on it.</u>

2 Wow! That's really big! Let's put it back the way it was. <u>Click on this Restore button.</u>

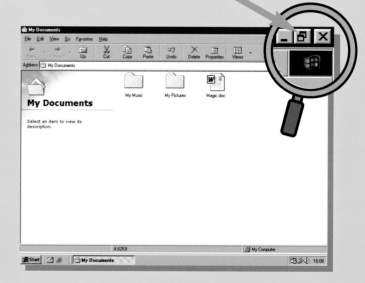

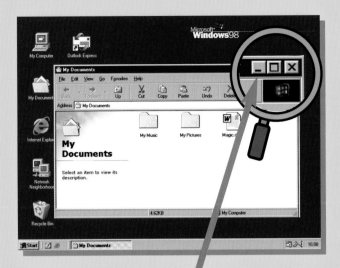

3 Here's a quick way to hide a window. Click on the Minimize button. Where does your window go?

4 Here it is! Click this button to put the window back into place.

Now practise opening and closing, and minimising and maximising other windows.

5 Ta-da! My Documents appears again, as if by magic!

13

Make a folder

Folders make it easy to keep your work organised. Let's find out how to make a new one!

 **1** We're going to make a folder inside My Documents. Click File, up here.

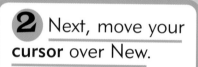 **2** Next, move your **cursor** over New.

3 Another **menu** opens! Now click on Folder.

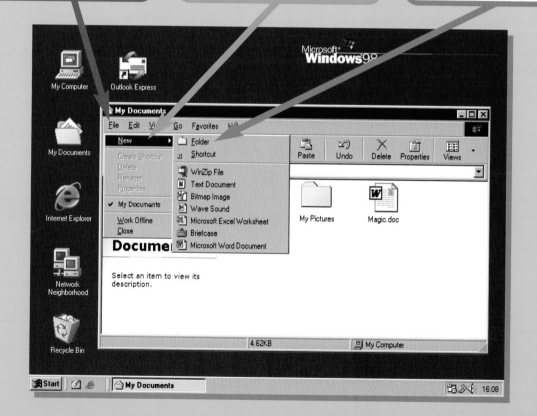

4 Your new folder magically appears!

5 Type a name for your folder and press Enter on your keyboard. We've typed the name 'Hocus Pocus'.

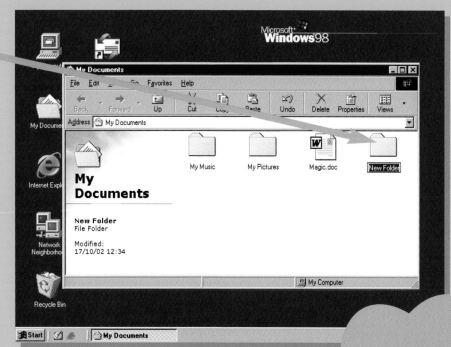

Try creating more folders on your computer. You could have one for your homework and one for your drawings.

Move it!

Let's move the Magic **document** into the Hocus Pocus **folder**. It's cut and paste magic!

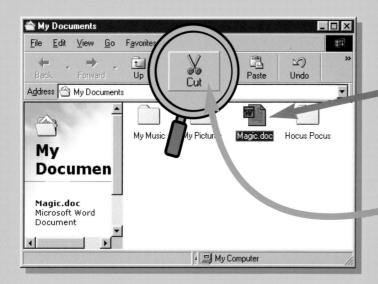

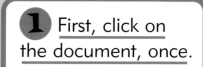

1 First, click on the document, once.

2 Next, click on this Cut button.

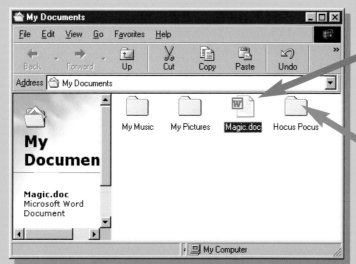

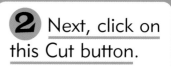

3 Spooky! Only a ghost of your document is left.

4 Double-click on the Hocus Pocus folder to open it.

5 Now click this Paste button to stick your Magic document into its new folder.

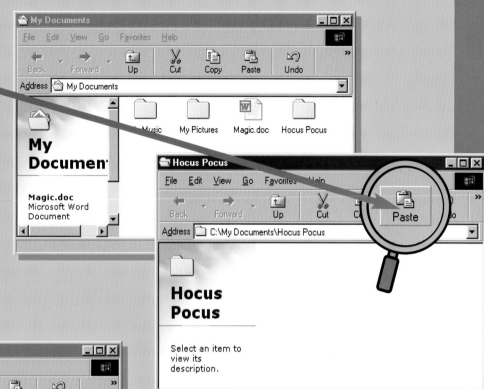

6 Abracadabra! The Magic document is in its new home.

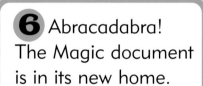

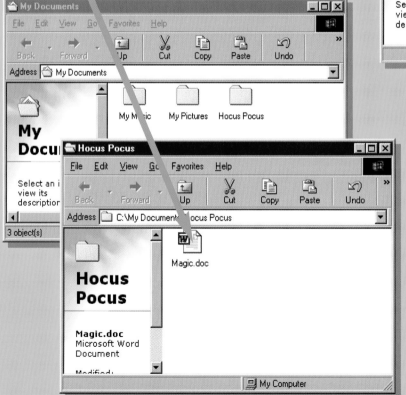

Hey presto!

Back in place

If you change your mind about a document you've just moved, don't worry. Just click the Undo button

↩
Undo

to put it back in place.

17

Copy that, copycat!

Let's make a copy of the Magic **document** and paste it into My Documents. It's double the fun!

1 First, click on the Magic document, once.

2 Next, click on the Copy button.

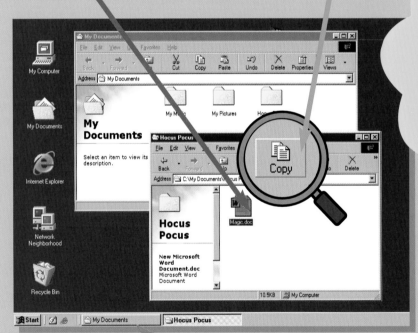

This time, your document doesn't disappear. But your computer knows you're going to paste it!

3 Now, open My Documents again. Click on this button.

Hey presto!

Folder vanishing trick!
Tidy up your Desktop in a flash by clicking this Desktop button.

Look for it in the bottom left-hand corner of your screen.

4 Find this Paste button and click on it.

5 Here it is! A perfect copy of your magic message!

19

Put it in the bin!

Keep your computer tidy by putting old **documents** into the Recycle bin.

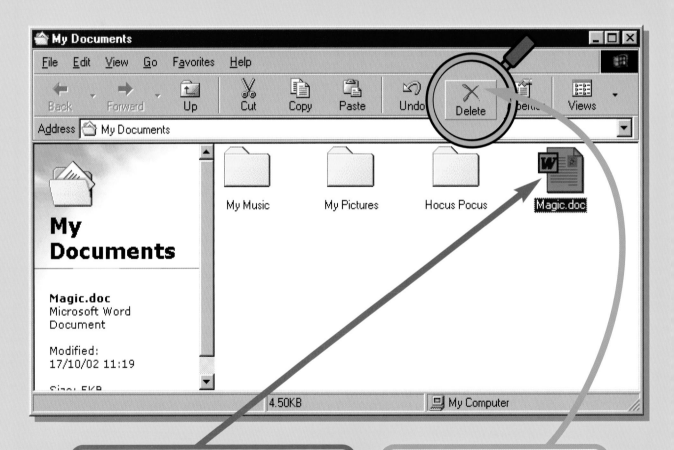

1 We've had enough of this Magic message. Let's throw it in the bin! Click on it, once.

2 Next, click on this Delete button. Delete means erase or rub out.

3 <u>Read this</u> question. Do you really want to throw away this document?

4 <u>Click the Yes</u> button to go ahead and put it in the bin.

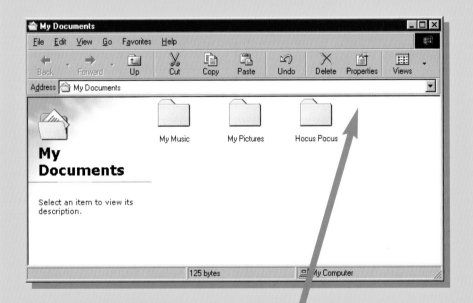

5 What a great vanishing trick! You can keep all your folders tidy this way.

Hey presto!

Quick delete
You can use your keyboard to delete documents, too. Click on the document, then press the Delete key on your keyboard. It looks like this...

Get it back!

Oops! What if you put a **document** in the bin by mistake? You can make it appear again in a flash!

1 Find the Recycle Bin on your desktop. <u>Then double-click on the Recycle Bin to open it.</u>

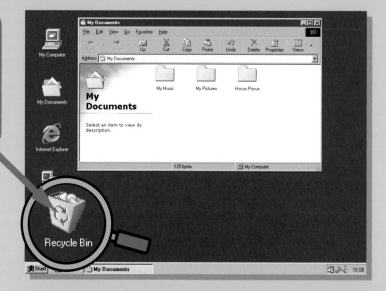

2 Sure enough, your document is in the bin! <u>Click on it.</u>

3 Move your **cursor** over <u>Restore</u> and click on it. Restore means put back.

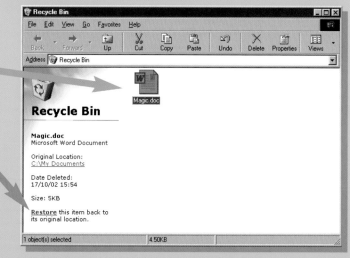

4 The Magic document has vanished from the Recycle Bin!

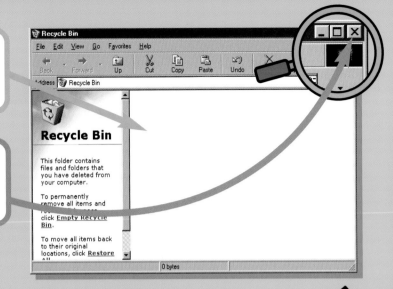

Recycle Bin

This folder contains files and folders that you have deleted from your computer.

To permanently remove all items and ~~click **Empty Recycle Bin**.~~

To move all items back to their original locations, click **Restore**

0 bytes

5 Now click here to close the Recycle Bin.

6 The Magic document is back where it started!

7 Click on the Minimize button to hide the window.

My Documents

My Music   My Pictures   Hocus Pocus   Magic.doc

My Documents

Select an item to view its description.

4.62KB   My Computer

Start   My Documents   16:08

Is there anything else you need to tidy up? Practise putting a folder in the Recycle Bin. Don't forget to restore it afterwards!

23

Time to decorate

This blue desktop is a bit boring. Let's give it extra sparkle with some wizard wallpaper!

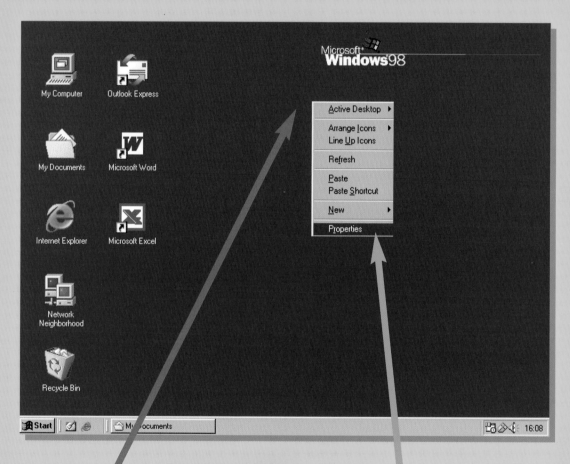

1 First, right-click on an empty part of the desktop.

2 A new **menu** pops up! Click on Properties.

3 Here's a list of wallpaper designs. Click the arrows to move up and down.

4 Choose a design and click on it.

5 You can see what it will look like, here.

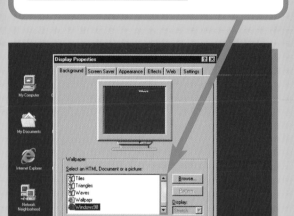

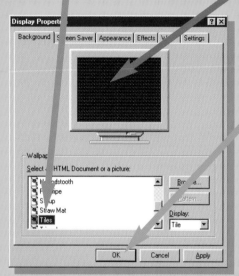

6 When you find one that you like, click on OK to choose it.

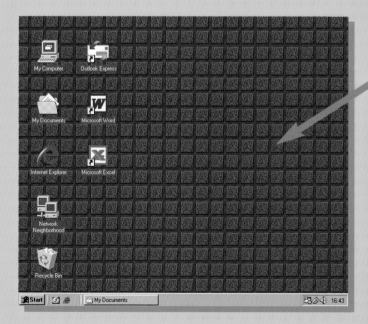

7 Your computer will look like this each time you use it!

Hey presto!

Swap it back
If you don't like your new wallpaper, just change it back! Follow steps 1-6. When you get to step 4, choose the wallpaper called Windows 98.

25

Super screen savers

Take a break from work and watch a screen saver on your computer. It's like a mini movie!

1 Right-click on an empty part of the desktop.

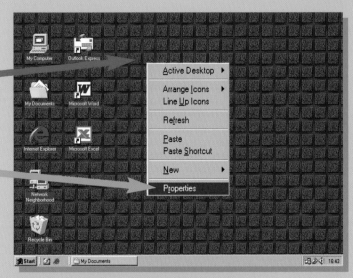

2 When a new **menu** appears, click Properties.

3 Click screen saver.

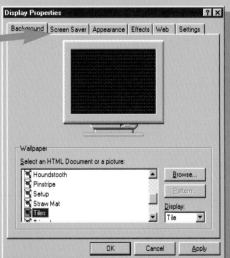

4 There's a list of screen savers, here. Click on one to see a sneak preview in the screen above.

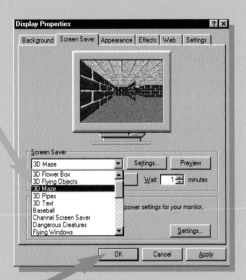

Hey presto!

Stop that screen saver! If you'd rather have no screen saver at all, just follow steps 1-6 again. When you get to step 4, find 'None' and click it.

5 When you've found a screen saver you like, click OK.

The screen saver plays when your computer is resting. Just move your mouse to make it stop.

6 Now leave your computer alone for a few minutes and see what happens!

Turn it off

When you've finished using your computer, you should turn it off in the right way. Here's how to do it.

1 First, click on the My Documents button at the bottom of your screen.

2 Next, close the window that pops up by clicking its Close button.

28

3 Now click the Start button.

4 Move your **cursor** up to Shut Down and click on it.

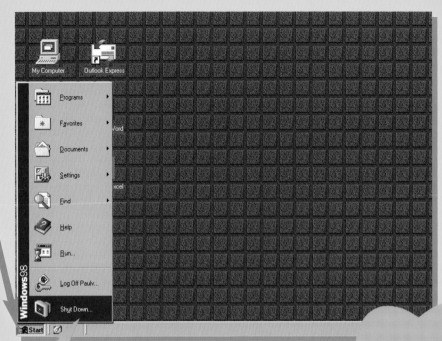

Programs
Favorites
Documents
Settings
Find
Help
Run...
Log Off Pauly...
Shut Down...

Windows98

Start

5 Click in the white circle next to Shut down to make a black dot appear.

6 Finish off by clicking on OK.

Shut Down Windows

What do you want the computer to do?

◯ Stand by
◉ Shut down
◯ Restart
◯ Restart in MS-DOS mode

OK   Cancel   Help

Your job is done! Your computer will shut down and turn itself off. See you later!

Guidance notes

Microsoft Windows '98 is the operating system for many computers. This book aims to show children how to take control of their computer and to find out about programs and folders.

Microsoft Windows
You can use this book with Microsoft Windows '95, '98, ME, 2000 and XP. There may be slight variations in buttons and toolbars between versions.

Macintosh users
This book is not compatible with Macintosh computers.

How to set up your computer

Children will find it easier to follow the steps in this book if their computer screen looks like the one in the book. Here's how to set up your computer to look like ours.

Your desktop
Set up your desktop with large icons and Windows '98 wallpaper.
❶ Right-click on an empty part of the desktop.
❷ Click Properties.
❸ Click on the Windows '98 wallpaper.
❹ Click the Effects tab.
❺ Make sure that Use large icons is ticked.
❻ Click OK.

Folders
Set the folder view to web and large icons.
❶ Open My Documents.
❷ Click the arrow next to the Views button.
❸ Make sure that 'Large Icons' and 'As Web Page' are ticked.
Now set your folder options to Classic.
❶ Click View on the menu bar.
❷ Click Folder Options.
❸ Make sure Classic Style is selected.
❹ Click OK.
Finally, make sure all folders are the same.
❶ Click View on the menu bar.
❷ Click Folder Options.
❸ Click the View tab.
❹ Click the 'Like current folder' button.
❺ Click Yes.
❻ Click OK.

Extension activities

Each chapter of Windows Magic is self-contained so children can learn at their own pace. Hey presto! boxes contain tips and ideas for extra practice. There are more extension activities below.

The Programs menu
Encourage children to explore the Programs menu on pages 6-7. As an extension activity, ask children to open other programs, such as Calculator, Paint, or even a game.

Individual folders

On pages 14-15, we make a new folder. Invite children to create folders with their own names. Show them how to find their folders in the Save As dialog box on page 9.

Folder games

Make a series of folders inside the My Documents folder and hide a document in one of them. The challenge is for the children to find the document, open it and then follow the instructions written in it. The instructions might be to delete the document (pages 20-21), or to move or copy it to another folder (pages 16-19).

Alternatively, send children on a computer treasure hunt through different documents and folders which eventually leads to the treasure. This might be a picture to print out.

Desktop designs

If you are working with children who share a computer, let them take turns to customise it with their favourite wallpaper and screen saver.

Make it fun!

Ask children about what they are doing and invite them to think about what they are going to do next. Encourage and praise them as they learn, and remember not to cover too much at once!

Health and safety

Supervise children when turning the computer on and off. Remind them not to put their fingers inside the computer at any time. Encourage them to take regular breaks to avoid repetitive strain injuries and eyestrain. Refer to the computer manual for information about the correct seating and posture. Children should be sitting upright with their feet on the floor and the keyboard in line with their elbows.

National Curriculum links for Information and Communication Technology

Key stage 1

Finding things out
- ✔ 1b. Entering and storing information in a variety of forms (for example, saving work).
- ✔ 1c. Retrieving information that has been stored (for example, loading saved work).

Developing ideas and making things happen
- ✔ 2c. Planning and giving instructions to make things happen.
- ✔ 2d. Trying things out and exploring what happens in real and imaginary situations.

Key stage 2

During Key Stage 2, pupils use a wider range of ICT tools and information sources to support their work in other subjects. In this book, children use Microsoft Windows to organise their work, launch different software programs and explore a range of ICT tools.
In particular, they learn to:
- ✔ 2a. Develop and refine ideas by bringing together, organising and reorganising text, tables, images and sound as appropriate.

Scottish National Guidelines 5-14 ICT

Strands covered at levels A and B
- ✔ Using the technology
- ✔ Creating and presenting

Useful words

computer program

A computer program helps you to do different jobs on your computer. This book is about a program called Microsoft Windows. Its job is to make your computer easy to use.

cursor

The cursor is what moves on your computer screen when you move your mouse. It can be different shapes, but often it's shaped like an arrow. You can use it to point to different parts of your screen.

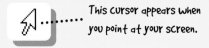

This cursor appears when you point at your screen.

folder

A computer folder is used for storing work, just like a real folder. In this book, you open the My Documents folder and make a new folder inside it.

menu

A computer menu is a list of things for you to choose, a bit like a menu in a restaurant!

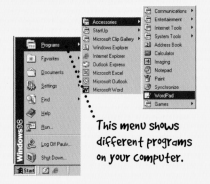

This menu shows different programs on your computer.

document

In this book, you open a program called WordPad and write a message to a friend. This message is called a document. Letters and stories are other examples of documents.

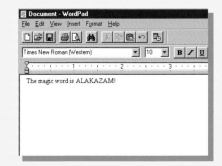

Index